SPOTLIGHT ON SOCIAL AND EMOTIONAL LEARNING

AN INNER DRIVE

SELF-MOTIVATION

CAITIE MCANENEY

PowerKiDS press™

NEW YORK

Published in 2020 by The Rosen Publishing Group, Inc.
29 East 21st Street, New York, NY 10010

Editor: Elizabeth Krajnik
Cover Design: Michael Flynn

Photo Credits: Cover, p. 15 Hero Images/Getty Images; cover, pp. 1, 3–4, 6, 8, 10, 12–14, 16, 18–24 (background) TairA/Shutterstock.com; p. 5 (main) ARIS MESSINIS/AFP/Getty Images; p. 5 (inset) Scott Barbour/Getty Images Sport/ Getty Images; p. 7 Asia Images Group/Shutterstock.com; p. 9 Prostock-studio/Shutterstock.com; p. 11 Sergey Novikov/ Shutterstock.com; p. 12 Justin Kirk Thornton/Shutterstock.com; p. 13 Billion Photos/Shutterstock.com; p. 17 Andy Lyons/Getty Images Sport/Getty Images; p. 18 Courtesy of the Library of Congress; p. 19 sirtravelalot/ Shutterstock.com; pp. 20–21 AlohaHawaii/Shutterstock.com; p. 22 Viacheslav Nikolaenko/Shutterstock.com.

Cataloging-in-Publication Data

Names: McAneney, Caitie.
Title: An inner drive: self-motivation / Caitie McAneney.
Description: New York : PowerKids Press, 2020. | Series: Spotlight on social and emotional learning | Includes glossary and index.
Identifiers: ISBN 9781725302051 (pbk.) | ISBN 9781725302242 (library bound) | ISBN 9781725302150 (6pack)
Subjects: LCSH: Motivation (Psychology)--Juvenile literature. | Personality and motivation--Juvenile literature.
Classification: LCC BF503.M39 2020 | DDC 153.8--dc23

Manufactured in the United States of America

CPSIA Compliance Information: Batch #CSPK19. For further information contact Rosen Publishing, New York, New York at 1-800-237-9932.

CONTENTS

CHAPTER ONE

TIME TO GET MOTIVATED!

Imagine you've got a basketball game that you want to win. Imagine you've got an important test coming up that you want to ace. How can you get from point A (where you're starting) to point B (achieving, or reaching, your goal)? It's time to get motivated!

Whenever you've got a big goal or task ahead, you need motivation, or the **desire** to achieve that goal. That's what drives you forward. It's like putting gas in the tank of a car. As long as the motivation doesn't run out, you won't give up on your goal, no matter what setbacks and **disappointments** may come your way.

Motivation works for tasks both big and small. Think of the motivation it takes for an **athlete** to make it to the Olympics. They have to practice and train for years and years, but their drive keeps them moving forward.

Trischa Zorn is a blind **Paralympic** swimmer for team USA who has won 55 medals, making her the most decorated Paralympian ever. Zorn has said, "My motivation lies in the fact that I truly love what I'm doing."

CHAPTER TWO

SKILLS FOR LIFE

Motivation is one part of the life skill of self-management. Self-management is the ability to control your actions, thoughts, and emotions in different situations. It's the difference between fighting a classmate over a problem and calmly working it out. It's also the difference between studying for an important test and playing video games all night. You have the power to manage your actions, and therefore, the outcomes.

Another skill of self-management includes managing stress, which is something that causes strong feelings of worry or anxiety. Many things in school and at home can cause stress. However, how you deal with stress is what matters most. **Impulse** control is a skill that has to do with rising above our **temporary** wants and urges, or strong desires, to achieve our longer-term goals. Lastly, self-management includes setting and working toward goals, even if you know they might take a while to achieve.

> Self-management is a social and emotional learning skill that helps you be a better friend, student, and family member.

CHAPTER THREE

YOU HAVE THE POWER!

The most important thing to remember when trying to stay motivated is that you have the power. You alone have power over your actions.

Imagine you want to learn to play the guitar. This takes a lot of time and practice. It takes motivation! However, your parents might not be able to afford music lessons. If that's the case, think of how you can take control of your situation. You might be able to borrow a guitar from school or you might be able to find instructional videos online. This can-do attitude, or way of thinking, can help you feel in control of the situation.

It's also important to remember that you have a choice in any situation. You can choose not to practice or you can practice hard. You can choose to give up or you can choose to keep going.

Sometimes it's hard to get motivated when you'd rather watch TV than practice or work. However, you have a choice. Do you want to give into short-term urges or achieve long-term goals?

CHAPTER FOUR

INTERESTS AND PASSIONS

What are you motivated to do? In other words, what do you want to do, without anyone telling you to do it? These things probably have to do with your interests and **passions**. These are things you care deeply about.

If you love to read, no one has to ask you twice to pick out a book at the library. If you love to play basketball, then nothing can keep you off the court. You're passionate about that hobby or task, so it doesn't really feel like work.

One way to get motivated to do something is to connect it to your interests or passions. Imagine you have to learn fractions in math class, but you don't really like math. However, you love to bake. You can connect baking to fractions to help get you motivated to learn!

Imagine you have to do community service for school. You can choose something you're passionate about, like a basketball **charity** event, to get you motivated!

CHAPTER FIVE

WHAT DRIVES YOU?

Think about the things that you've achieved in your life. Maybe you've earned a purple belt in karate or organized a canned-food drive. What was driving you to do that task? Did you do it because you had to, or because you wanted to?

There are two types of motivation—extrinsic and intrinsic. Extrinsic motivation is a driving force from outside yourself that leads you to do something to avoid punishment or gain a reward. You clean your room to avoid being grounded. Extrinsic motivation helps you achieve short-term success.

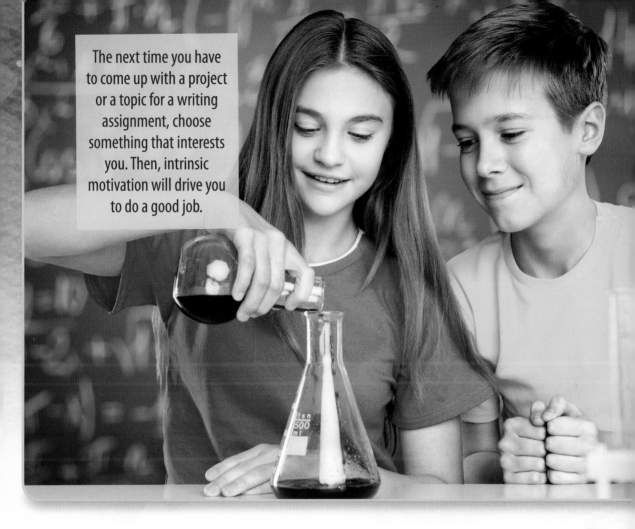

The next time you have to come up with a project or a topic for a writing assignment, choose something that interests you. Then, intrinsic motivation will drive you to do a good job.

Intrinsic motivation is a driving force from within yourself that makes you do something because you want to. You might do a science project on mountain lions because they are your favorite animals, and it excites you to learn about them. Extrinsic motivation works, but intrinsic motivation keeps working in the long run.

CHAPTER SIX

THE STEPS TO SUCCESS

You might have trouble getting motivated because you're not sure where to start with a task. Follow these steps and you'll be on your way to achieving your goal.

The first step is setting your goal. This might seem easy, but it's important to make sure your goal is **specific** and **realistic**. For example, you might say your goal is to save money. But how do you do that? Be realistic. It's more realistic to save $100 than $1 million. Be specific. If you want to earn money for a new video game, you might set a goal to save $60.

Write down your goal. With long-term goals, it can be hard to see the finish line. That makes it easy to give up. When you write down your goal, you can look at it from time to time and make a plan to achieve it.

With your specific and realistic goal to save $60, you'll have to do things to make money. You might rake your neighbors' lawns, do extra chores around the house, or start a lemonade stand to achieve your goal.

CHAPTER SEVEN

SMALL STEPS AND LITTLE VICTORIES

It's hard to get motivated when the challenge in front of you seems too big to tackle. Tackling that big task might be impossible, so why even try?

Any big problem or task can be broken down into many smaller parts. You don't have to write an entire story in one sitting. You can write a story one small part at a time. You won't win a swimming medal if you don't even know how to swim. First, you have to learn to swim, then swim a lap, then swim 10 laps, then join a team, and then compete. Breaking a goal down into smaller steps makes it accessible, or able to be reached. With **self-discipline**, you will keep working on each small goal to achieve a big goal.

It's important to celebrate little victories as well. Give yourself credit when you complete an important step or reach a new level.

World-champion runner Kara Goucher, pictured here, once said, "**Acknowledge** all of your small victories. They will **eventually** add up to something great."

CHAPTER EIGHT

OVERCOMING OBSTACLES

Often, when someone is faced with an obstacle, or challenge, their first thought is that they want to give up, which can make it hard to stay motivated. This is because many people think success is a straight line. Really, there are many twists and turns on the way to achieving your goals. When you've accepted that there will be obstacles, you can figure out how to overcome them.

President Barack Obama, pictured here, said, "If you run you stand a chance of losing, but if you don't run you've already lost."

Imagine your goal is to score a home run for your baseball team. You're motivated. You've trained hard with your teammates. Then, during a game, the other team's outfielder catches the ball you just hit. This is an obstacle between you and your goal. You could give up—or you could keep trying. When you keep trying in the face of challenges, you become **resilient**. Get comfortable with the chance of failure, and you'll be able to stay motivated no matter what comes your way!

CHAPTER NINE

WHEN YOU DON'T FEEL LIKE IT

Have you ever started to do something and thought, "I just don't feel like it"? It could be something that's not that interesting to you, such as math homework. It could even be something you enjoy doing, such as playing the guitar. Either way, that task is unappealing to you at the moment.

If you lose your motivation, it might help to give some more thought to your goal. Think of all you've achieved so far, forgive yourself for slipping up, and make a plan to get back on track.

Take a minute to think about why you don't feel motivated. Maybe you're feeling tired or sad. Maybe you don't believe in yourself. Once you identify these feelings, you can start to overcome them.

Sometimes we aren't motivated because we don't think a task is meaningful. You might feel like there's no reason for you to do your homework. However, you can think of your homework as a part of a bigger goal, like getting into college. Doing this task will have more meaning and you'll feel more motivated.

CHAPTER TEN

WHAT IS YOUR "WHY"?

Many things can get in the way of your goals. You might not have the resources, or things you need, to achieve your goals. You might not have a lot of time to practice. You might be tired. At these times, it's your inner drive that keeps you going. Purpose fuels your inner drive.

Ask yourself: "Why do I want to do this? What is the purpose?" If you want to try out for a play, your "why" might be because you love to act. Acting in this play will bring you joy.

Your purpose will remind you why it's important to overcome obstacles or feelings of boredom or fear. It will remind you why self-management and self-discipline are important, especially when it comes to controlling your actions. Find your "why" and you'll never lose your drive.

GLOSSARY

acknowledge (ihk-NAH-lihj) To make known that something has been received or noticed.

athlete (ATH-leet) A person who is trained in or good at games and exercises that require physical skill, endurance, and strength.

charity (CHAR-uh-tee) An organization that helps people or animals.

desire (dih-ZY-uhr) A feeling of wanting something or to do something.

disappointment (dis-uh-POYNT-muhnt) Someone or something that doesn't meet your hopes or expectations.

eventually (eh-VEHNT-shoo-uh-lee) At some later time or in the end.

impulse (IHM-puhls) A sudden strong desire to do something.

Paralympic (pehr-uh-LIHM-pihk) Having to do with a series of international contests for athletes with disabilities.

passion (PAH-shuhn) An object of someone's love, liking, or desire.

realistic (ree-uh-LIH-stik) Ready to see things as they really are and to deal with them sensibly.

resilient (rih-ZIHL-yuhnt) Having the ability to recover from or adjust to misfortune or change.

self-discipline (SELHF–DIH-suh-pluhn) The ability to make yourself do things that should be done.

specific (spih-SIH-fik) Clearly and exactly presented or stated.

temporary (TEHM-puh-rehr-ee) Lasting for a limited time.

INDEX

PRIMARY SOURCE LIST

Page 5
Trischa Zorn of USA in action while winning a silver medal in the women's 100m breaststroke final at the Sydney International Aquatic Centre during the Sydney 2000 Paralympic Games, Sydney, Australia. Photograph. Scott Barbour. October 22, 2000. ALLSPORT.

Page 17
Kara Goucher runs in the women's 5,000 meter during day four of the 2015 USA Outdoor Track & Field Championships at Hayward Field in Eugene, Oregon. Photograph. Andy Lyons. June 28, 2015. Getty Images Sport.

Page 18
Official portrait of President Barack Obama in the Oval Office. Photograph. Pete Souza. December 6, 2012. Now kept in the Library of Congress Prints and Photographs Division, Washington, D.C.

WEBSITES

Due to the changing nature of Internet links, PowerKids Press has developed an online list of websites related to the subject of this book. This site is updated regularly. Please use this link to access the list: www.powerkidslinks.com/SSEL/drive